PUBLIC LIBRARY
301 S. Market
OSKALOOSA, IA 52577

WITHDRAWN

SEQUOIA AND KINGS CANYON

BY
Maxine McCormick

I wish to thank Lisa Okazaki, Park Ranger at Sequoia/Kings Canyon National Parks, Paul Tackes, Seasonal Ranger/Naturalist at Sequoia National Park, and George Shaw, Associate Professor of Geophysics at the University of Minnesota for all their help. Special thanks to the people at the Sequoia Natural History Association who provided me with the materials that made this book possible.

PUBLISHED BY
CRESTWOOD HOUSE
Mankato, MN, U.S.A.

LIBRARY OF CONGRESS CATALOGING IN PUBLICATION DATA

McCormick, Maxine.
  Sequoia and Kings Canyon

  (National parks)
  Includes index.
  SUMMARY: Describes the history, geography, and plant and animal life of these two national parks that are located next to each other in California. Also includes a park map.
  1. Sequoia National Park (Calif.) — Juvenile literature. 2. Kings Canyon National Park (Calif.) — Juvenile literature. [1. Sequoia National Park (Calif.) 2. Kings Canyon National Park (Calif.) 3. National parks and reserves.] I. Title.
F868.S4M37   1988   979.4'86—dc19   88-20214
ISBN 0-89686-409-X

International Standard Book Number:
0-89686-409-X

Library of Congress Catalog Card Number:
88-20214

PHOTO CREDITS

Cover: Tom Stack & Associates: John Gerlach
Paul Tackes: 12-13, 22-23, 25, 27, 31, 32, 43
DRK Photo: (NH (Dan) Cheatham) 7, 17, 18; (Wayne Lynch) 9, 30; (Paul Von Baich) 14
Tom Stack & Associates: (Tom Stack) 4; (John Gerlach) 11, 34, 35, 37, 40-41; (Jeff Foott) 24; (D. Jorgenson) 28; (Tom Algire) 21

Copyright © 1988 by Crestwood House, Inc. All rights reserved. No part of this book may be reproduced in any form without written permission from the publisher, except for brief passages included in a review. Printed in the United States of America.

Produced by Carnival Enterprises.

Box 3427, Mankato, MN, U.S.A. 56002

TABLE OF CONTENTS

The Giant Bear And The Great Discovery..5
The Lumbermen And The Big Trees..6
The Saving Of The Sequoias..8
Born Of Fire..10
From Seedling To Giant..15
Living Fossils...16
Meet The Generals...18
The First People...19
What Is The Mountain Forest Like?..20
The Ouzel And The Golden Trout..24
Where Did The Mountains Come From?..26
What Shapes A Mountain?..29
Climbing Mount Whitney..30
What Is It Like On Top Of A Mountain?..33
In Giant Forest...33
Moro Rock...36
Crystal Cave..38
How To Be Safe In The Mountains..38
Things To Do...42
Saying Goodbye And Hello..42
For More Park Information...44
Park Map...45
Glossary/Index...46-47

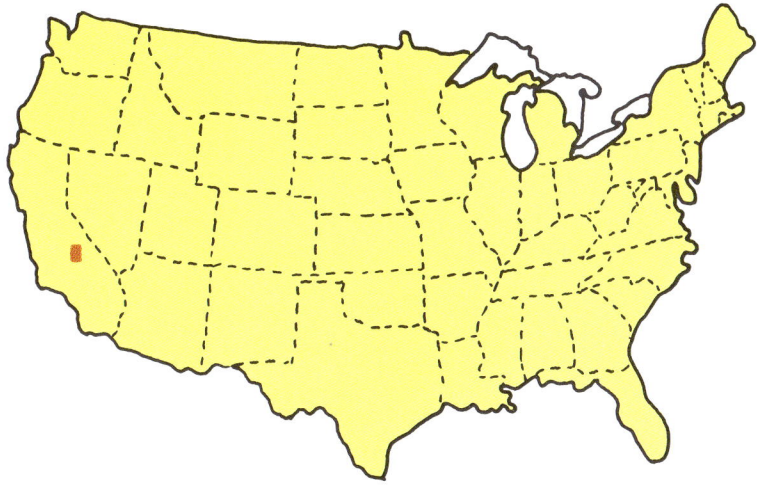

Sequoia and Kings Canyon National Parks

THE GIANT BEAR AND THE GREAT DISCOVERY

One day in 1852, a hunter named A.T. Dowd shot and wounded a grizzly bear. He was hunting for meat for a gold-mining camp in California. The bear fled and Dowd chased him over miles of mountain country.

All at once, Dowd realized he was standing in front of a gigantic tree. It was as wide as a house and rose so tall he could not see the top of it. The lowest branch was 100 feet from the ground. That branch alone was as big as an ordinary tree.

Dowd stared at the stupendous tree. He forgot all about the grizzly. Who would believe such a tree? He touched the rough bark and walked around it just to prove he wasn't dreaming. He looked about. There were more!

Dowd couldn't wait to tell the camp of his discovery. Of course, they all laughed. Tall tales were popular in those days—everyone tried to tell the most fantastic story. No one would believe Dowd.

So Dowd gave up his story and didn't say anymore. Then one Sunday morning, he rushed into camp and announced loudly that he had just shot the largest grizzly bear he had ever seen in his life. The dead bear was in

Sequoia trees are the largest living things on Earth.

the forest and he needed help bringing it back.

Everyone loved grizzly steaks. They were delicious. So the whole camp turned out to help bring back the gigantic bear.

Dowd led them through the forest, down deep canyons, up steep ridges, until finally they rounded a bend. There was his tree, just as he had described it. It was an overpowering sight. The men stood dumbfounded staring at the tree. "Now do you believe my big tree story?" Dowd yelled. "This is the big grizzly bear I wanted you to see."

The miners gathered around the tree, touching its knobby base. They leaned way back and squinted up at its towering crown. Now they believed! After this, the trees became famous.

Word spread. Kings, presidents, dukes, and rich people from all over came to see the giant trees. Everyone who saw them was astonished. Newspapers spread the story. But people who could not see the sequoias did not believe such giants were real.

So the bark of one was peeled off and put on display in New York. Thousands of people came to stare. The rest of the tree was left in the forest to die slowly, without its bark to protect it.

Soon lumbermen began cutting the trees down. Others realized that these ancient giants needed help if they were to survive.

Why is the sequoia so special? If a sequoia grew in a city it would completely fill the street. It would tower as tall as a 26-story building. They are the largest living things on earth. They are one of the oldest living things, too. Some are 3,000 years old.

Today, they are protected in the Sierra Nevada Mountains of eastern California. These mountains have been their home for more than two million years. The largest groves are found in Sequoia and Kings Canyon National Parks. These two parks are nestled side by side in the mountains. Their duty is to care for the giant trees.

THE LUMBERMEN AND THE BIG TREES

In the 1850s, people rushed into California in search of gold. Cities sprouted up. Schools, churches, stores, everything had to be built to care for

FUN FACT The name "Sequoia gigantea" was first used by Stephen Endlicher, an Austrian botanist in 1847. Seven years later, that name was again used by a French botanist Joseph Decaisne to identify the giant trees of the Sierra Nevada. Since then, this has been their name.

When a sequoia tree has fallen, many men are needed to move it.

all the immigrants. They needed wood.

Lumber companies quickly claimed the land where the big sequoias stood. But logging these monstrous trees proved quite a task. Lumbermen built a high platform against the base of the tree. They did not want to cut into the thickest part of the trunk.

Before cutting, they took measurements to see if the tree was growing straight, or if it leaned. If it fell the wrong way, it would shatter. A trench was dug and lined with small trees and branches to cushion the tree's fall.

Then two men with axes mounted the platform and began chopping. They chopped till they were halfway through the tree. It took many days. Finally they used a 25-foot cross-cut saw to cut through from the other side.

The wood of the giant sequoia was very brittle. Because no one could quite control 4,000 tons of tree as it came thundering down, most of the trees shattered when they fell. The sections were so big they had to be dynamited

FUN FACT The Spanish words "sierra nevada" mean "saw-toothed" and "snowy." The Spanish explorers who first saw the range described it on a map in 1776 as "una gran sierra nevada," a great snow-covered mountain range.

to break them apart.

The broken sections were milled to be used as roof shingles, vineyard stakes (for grapes), and fence posts. But one tree could make more than 100,000 board feet of timber. The lumbermen kept cutting. They destroyed a lot of trees before they could be stopped.

THE SAVING OF THE SEQUOIAS

A storm of protest rose over the destruction of the sequoias. People felt it a tragedy that these noble giants were being cut down for fence posts and pencils for Europe. More than half of every tree was wasted. The top and much of the trunk were left to rot on the ground.

John Muir, a man who loved the forest, decided to help. He wanted to see how many groves were left. He was afraid lumber companies would claim all the groves and cut them down before they could be saved.

One day in August 1875, Muir set out from Yosemite Valley in the northern part of the Sierra Nevada Mountains. He carried no gun. He was not afraid of hunger or danger. He loved to roam and he was curious about everything. Muir was blinded in one eye in a mill accident when he was young. From that time on he decided to spend the rest of his life exploring the wilderness.

"As long as I live," he wrote, "I'll hear waterfalls and birds and winds sing. I'll interpret the rocks, learn the language of flood, storm, and the avalanche. I'll...get as near the heart of the world as I can."

On this trip alone, Muir walked nearly 200 miles. All through the mountains he found groves of sequoia. Finally, after many weeks, he came to "a magnificent growth of giants." At night, he lay on his back staring up at the stars through their colossal heads. To him it seemed the stars sparkled on their branches like flowers. He named this grove the Giant Forest. Today, it is part of Sequoia National Park.

It took a long time to make this area a park. Lumber companies wanted the trees. People in the dry valley wanted the rights to the rivers and lakes. Ranchers wanted to graze their herds in the mountain meadows. Congress

Many magnificent sequoias grow in Giant Forest.

was slow to act.

In September of 1890, Sequoia finally became a national park. It was the second national park in the United States (Yellowstone was the first). A week later Grant Grove, a tiny area near Sequoia, was made a park, too. Through the years more land was added to Sequoia. But it wasn't until 1940 that Kings Canyon was made a national park. This was 88 years after the discovery of the big trees.

Sequoia is 604 square miles. Kings Canyon, which lies next to it, is 710 square miles. Within these parks live most of the giant trees. Strangely enough, however, by saving the trees people exposed them to still other dangers.

BORN OF FIRE

In the early days, the U.S. cavalry managed the national parks. One of their jobs was to stop the spread of fire. They wanted to keep the parks safe so people would visit them.

Then in 1960, a college student made an important discovery. While looking at some old photographs of a sequoia grove, he was shocked to find that the grove looked sunny and open. Seedlings and young sequoia trees were everywhere.

The forest he knew had become dark and overgrown. It was shaded by so much plant growth that new sequoia trees could not grow.

Now scientists know that fire is important to the trees. How? Fire burns away twigs, needles, and branches that cover the pine forest floor. It cleans up the soil so it is free of disease that could harm new seedlings. Fire kills rot and insects that might harm the trees. The ash from a fire is rich in minerals that new plants need.

Fire also burns up other kinds of shade trees. This opens up the area for the sun-loving seedlings of the sequoia. But most important, it drys the cones that have been hanging in trees for years. Then billions of new seeds can fall to the ground. They fall into rich ashes that help them grow.

Since that discovery, the parks have started a program of *controlled burnings*. This means they start fires on purpose.

First rangers decide where they need the fire. They look for rocks and meadows and trails that will help contain it. They plan a fire that is hot enough to burn quickly, but not too hot to harm the trees.

Rangers use "controlled burnings" to create a healthy environment for new sequoia seedlings.

They clear away branches from the base of the trees so the fire won't burn too long or too hot and damage the trees. When the wind and moisture in the air are just right, they start the fire.

People are shocked when they first see a grove that has been burned. The trees are black. The ground is covered with white ashes and fallen logs. Some logs smolder for months until rain or snow finally puts them out.

But this "black death" will be the life of countless new trees. Before there were parks, lightning caused many fires. That was nature's way of helping. Sequoias have thick bark—some two feet thick—that protects them. If they are scarred from fire, they can heal themselves and grow new bark.

Soon after a fire, the sequoias will drop billions of new seeds into the cleared soil. In the spring there will be a surprise. Wild plants creep between the trees and cover the ground with colorful flowers. Thousands of inch-tall baby sequoias will be growing among those flowers.

In ten years most of the signs of the fire are gone. The scorched bark has flaked away. The forest litter is thick again. Scattered through the sun-filled forest are blue-green saplings of young sequoias. These young trees are the future, and fire makes it happen.

Visitors to Sequoia and Kings Canyon are treated to breathtaking scenery.

FROM SEEDLING TO GIANT

Fire, a tiny beetle, and the Douglas squirrel all help the sequoia to survive. A mature tree may have 11,000 or more cones hanging in its crown. There are about 200 winged seeds in each ripe cone. The seed is paper thin, no bigger than a little fingernail or a flake of oatmeal. With the help of fire, cones dry out, open up, and the seeds fall.

The Douglas squirrel, also called a chickaree, helps too. It is a small, noisy, fast-moving creature. It has a grey back, a light-colored belly, and a white ring around each eye.

The Douglas squirrel hates sequoia seeds but loves the fiber inside the cone. It scampers up a tree and busily cuts the cones down. Someone once saw one squirrel cut down 539 cones in 31 minutes! Then it scampered down to carry them one by one to its storehouse beneath the tree. As it eats, it tears open the cone and the seeds fall to the ground.

There is a tiny beetle that helps, too. Beetle larvae chew their way into the cone and eat the tissue inside. The cone dries out, and the seeds fall to the ground.

If the seed is good, it quickly roots. By autumn the *seedling* may have six tiny branches and be four inches high. It has a *tap root* to help it find water.

By the second year, it is 8 to 12 inches tall. It loves the sun, and if it has rooted in a good spot, it will grow. If it has fallen near another tree, the shade may kill it.

In ten years it is the size and shape of a Christmas tree. Its branches go all the way to the ground. It has a pointed top.

In 100 years it may be 150 feet tall. The trunk is four feet thick. The tap root is gone and the roots now spread out 100 feet or more under the ground. It still has a pointed top. Some of its lower branches have fallen off. The bark has a purple tinge to it.

After 500 years it thrusts out huge limbs that grow upward, reaching for the sun. It has a dome shape on top and its foliage grows in cloudlike tufts.

At 1,000 years all the lower branches are gone. It has survived roaring fires and heavy snow. The trunk may be 20 feet thick. It is now a cinnamon-red color. The tree is 250 to 300 feet tall.

By the time it is 2,000 or 3,000 years old, lightning has killed some of the top branches. It has a craggy look. It may be deeply scarred or even hollowed out by fire. Still it stands, a ton of foliage at its top.

1,000-year-old sequoias are about 250 feet tall and have lost all of their lower branches.

Sequoias are seldom bothered by insects or disease. They have something in their bark called tannin. It helps protect them and keeps them from rotting. Sequoia logs can lie on the ground for 500 years and still not rot.

The sequoia's weakness is its roots. They are shallow and spread out. A mountain stream can *erode* the soil around them. Still its straight, thick trunk makes it very hard to topple.

But fire can sometimes kill part of the trunk and roots and cause the tree to lean. With its great weight, a leaning tree is in trouble. In the spring when the ground is soft, it can fall. A heavy winter snow-load on the crown may bring it down.

LIVING FOSSILS

Fossil records show that ancient relatives of the sequoia appeared on the earth more than 100 million years ago. They lived when the dinosaurs thundered over the earth.

Fossils have been found in Greenland, France, England, and Asia. In our country, there is an ancient *petrified forest* in Yellowstone Park in Wyoming. In it are old sequoia logs that have turned to stone. Fossils have also been found in Texas, Pennsylvania, and Nevada.

Twenty-five million years ago, relatives of the sequoia grew in thick forests over the earth. Why are there so few left? Huge sheets of glaciers wiped out most of them. The cold that spread over the earth made it impossible for them to grow. The forests shrank.

As the Sierra Nevada Mountains rose, the trees found a place where it was neither too hot or too cold. There was just enough moisture. The Sierra Nevada has been home to the sequoia for the last two million years. Only 75 groves are left scattered through the mountains.

They grow in the middle range of the mountains on large, flat ridges where the soil can hold plenty of water even in the dry months of the summer.

The sequoias are like living fossils. They are the remains of a prehistoric plant that once covered the earth and is now almost extinct.

The monstrous sequoias have only one weakness—their shallow roots.

MEET THE GENERALS

The General Sherman tree is the largest living thing on earth. This means it has the most bulk, or mass, of any living thing. It was named by James Wolverton in 1879. He was a cattleman and trapper. He named it for William T. Sherman, his commander in the Civil War. It grows in the Giant Forest of Sequoia Park.

The General Sherman is as high as the Capitol Dome in Washington, D.C. The amount of wood in its trunk could build 40 five-room houses. It would take 30 railroad cars just to haul the trunk alone.

The General Sherman tree is as tall as the Capital Dome in Washington, D.C.

The General Grant tree is the third largest living thing on earth. It was found by Joseph H. Thomas in 1862. It was named for Ulysses S. Grant by Lucretia Baker.

The General Grant is the Nation's Christmas Tree. It also is a national shrine for all those who have been killed in war. It grows in Grant Grove in Kings Canyon Park.

THE FIRST PEOPLE

Prehistoric people lived in and near the parks a thousand years ago. But not much is known about them. They left behind arrow points and *pictographs* (pictures painted on rock).

The Monache or Western Mono were the people living in the parks when white people came.

The Mono built cone-shaped homes that they dug a foot or two into the ground. They covered the tops and sides with willow or cedar bark. They also made smaller buildings to store acorns.

Acorns were their main food. They gathered them in the fall and pounded them with *hammerstones* to remove the shells. Then the women would grind the acorns into meal in *mortars*. The mortars were holes worn deep into large flat rocks.

The meal was then placed in a shallow basin and water was poured over it. This helped remove the acorn's bitter taste.

They cooked the meal in a waterproof cooking basket. A stone, hot from the fire, was dropped in and kept in motion so it would not burn through the basket. The hot stone cooked the meal. When it was done, the acorn meal was eaten as a mush.

The Mono hunted with bows and arrows. Mule deer was a favorite meat. They trapped weasels, squirrels, rabbits, and other small animals. Fishing was plentiful. At times they hunted bear and mountain sheep.

The women were excellent basket makers. Baskets were used for everything, even as dishes. They made seed baskets, mush-cooking baskets, and baskets for water. They also had treasure baskets. They even wove cradles for their babies.

They traded with the desert people east of the mountains. The Mono got pine nuts, dried larvae of flies taken from the salt lakes, and salt. They also

FUN FACT Arrowheads scattered about the parks are signs that prehistoric people knew of and used the mountains as long ago as 2,000 years.

got rabbitskin blankets and *obsidian*. They used this rock to make arrowheads. In trade, they gave the desert people acorn meal, shell beads, deer skins, and arrow shafts.

The Mono were a gentle, family-minded people, careful of their natural world. The mountains were their home. They lived in them for hundreds of years. They left the mountains as they found them. Except for the trails, there is little to show that they were ever there.

WHAT IS THE MOUNTAIN FOREST LIKE?

In parts of the park, thick forests grow. Ponderosa pine with its golden bark and the sequoia with its cinnamon-red bark tower together. Both grow up to 200 feet high. Fir and sugar pine live here, too. Sugar pines can reach 200 feet, also.

Ponderosa pine is called yellow pine because of the color of its bark. John Muir once said he could tell when he was in this part of the forest because of the fine "music" of the yellow pine. What he liked was the hum of the wind high in the tops of the tall trees.

Black oak grows in dry areas of the forest. Its acorns were once a rich source of food for the Native Americans. They shared this food with the acorn woodpecker. The acorn woodpecker drills thousands of holes in other trees, buildings, and fence posts. When the acorns are ripe, it removes them from the oak and hammers them into the holes.

In years past when the harvest was poor, the Native Americans would raid the supplies put away by the acorn woodpecker. Black bears, mule deer, pigeons, jays, and squirrels also eat the acorns.

Summer in the forest is warm and dry. The winter is cool and snowy. As much as 200 inches of snow can fall. The sequoia gets it water from this snow. In the spring, the snow melts and seeps into the ground.

One of the very first plants to poke its head out of the ground after the snow melts is the snow plant. It has no green leaves; therefore, it cannot make its own food. The plant depends on rotting matter to help it grow.

The snow plant has a thick, bright-red, fleshy stem, and small red flowers

FUN FACT The Bear's Bathtub is not a tree. It is a hollow formed by the bases of two living trees. It is about three feet deep and is usually filled with water. There is a story about this hollow. One day an old guide named Chester Wright came upon a bear bathing in the pool. No one knows who was more surprised, Chester or the bear!

Giant sequoias have withstood warm, dry summers and heavy winter snowfalls.

In the springtime, yellow-throated gilias bloom and grow throughout Sequoia and Kings Canyon National Parks.

on top. It grows up to 15 inches high. It looks something like fat asparagus, but it isn't green.

In the springtime, the meadows and valley are filled with wildflowers. Orange tiger lilies bloom in the meadows. Gooseberries, thimbleberries, and wild roses seek the shade of the tall trees.

In sunny spots between the trees, mountain misery carpets the ground.

FUN FACT The General Sherman is 2,300 to 2,700 years old. It is 274 feet tall. The height of its first branch is 130 feet off the ground. The distance around its trunk at the ground is 102 feet.

It has tiny white flowers. The Native Americans called it kit-kit-dizze. They made a tea to use as a medicine from its leaves.

Yellow-throated gilia, tall purple lupine, popcorn flowers, and yellow primrose grow in the forest next to the giant trees. In once-burned places, these flowers crowd the ground. Animals come back, too. Mule deer, black bear, and other animals feed on new green shoots. They eat the buds, leaves,

FUN FACT The General Grant is 1,800 to 2,000 years old. It is 267 feet tall. The height of its first branch is 129 feet. The distance around the trunk at the ground is 107 feet.

and bark of small trees and other green plants.

There are many birds. Bluebirds, robins, and violet-green swallows sing in the meadows and make their nests in the trees. The red-tailed hawk soars high above, seeking its prey. Lizards and snakes sun themselves among the rocks.

THE OUZEL AND THE GOLDEN TROUT

Two animals are special to the parks and the mountains. They are the *ouzel* (pronounced OO-zel) and the golden trout.

The ouzel is a bird that loves waterfalls. It builds its nest close by so the spray will keep it moist. The nest is shaped like a beehive, with a little arched opening at the bottom. It is made of green and yellow moss. The moss on

Ouzels brave near-freezing water to feed in streams and lakes.

Golden trout flourish in the deep, quiet waters of the Kern River.

the outside stays fresh and green.

On dark days or sunny days, in snow or strong wind, the ouzel is out looking for food. It is always singing.

It eats water insects and loves the larvae of mosquitos. It walks upstream in the shallow water, sticking its head below the surface to turn over pebbles looking for food. If it can't find any, it flies over to deeper water and dives below the surface. There it walks about on the bottom doing the same thing.

In the winter when the land is snowbound and the streams are covered with slush and ice, the ouzel dives into a near-freezing lake. After two or three minutes it bursts into the air. It flies to a rock and sings a cheerful song. Then back it goes to the bottom of the lake. If the current gets too strong, it simply spreads its wings and "flies."

John Muir described this bird as a "joyous and lovable little fellow…

FUN FACT   The ouzel is now known as the American Dipper.

smoothly plump and compact as a pebble that has been whirled in a pothole."

High in the mountains, in a quiet, deep pool a golden trout waits for something delicious to float by. The golden trout is found in the Kern River in the southern part of the mountains. It was cut off from other trout thousands of years ago.

Slowly, it took on the color of the yellow mud and reddish sand in the steam bed. Its sides are yellow-to-rich gold and its belly is bright red. Its back and tail are green. The back is speckled with black dots.

In 1876, a lumberman carried a coffeepot full of them to the sawmill where he worked. He dumped them into the Cottonwood Creek. He hoped they would give him good sport. Since then they have been placed in many different lakes and streams to see if they can live and have young.

Like the ouzel, the golden trout is special. Both add color and wonder to their mountain water *habitat*.

Several large animals make their homes in the parks. Mule deer, black bear, and mountain lions live in the forests. Mountain sheep prefer the highest peaks, far from humans. In winter when it snows, many animals and birds move lower down the mountain to find food.

WHERE DID THE MOUNTAINS COME FROM?

Two hundred million years ago, there used to be an inland sea where the Sierra Nevada Mountains now stand. On the western side of the sea, a huge mountain range rose many thousands of feet into the sky. Over time, these mountains eroded. Sand, mud, and shells and bones of sea animals piled up at the bottom of the sea. These layers were thousands of feet thick. There was so much pressure that the layers changed into rock.

Much later, great forces in the earth folded and crumpled the rock and forced it up into a new mountain. During this time of mountain building, *magma,* or liquid rock, pushed up beneath the mountain range. When it cooled, it formed a huge *granite* block. This block is called a *batholite*. It is 400 miles long and about 60 miles wide. Over time this mountain range also eroded away, but the granite block remained.

Ten million years ago, the block of granite began to tilt upward on

The Sierra Nevada Mountains took many thousands of years to form.

Glaciers cut deep valleys into the mountains.

the east side. Earthquakes shook the area causing the block to rise inch by inch, foot by foot, higher and higher. Today, that granite block is the Sierra Nevada Range.

It took four major *upthrusts* and many smaller ones to get the Sierra Nevada Range as high as it is today. In between were great periods of calm. Then rivers did their work. They cut deep, steep-walled *valleys*. Kings Canyon is 8,000 feet deep in places. It is one of the deepest *canyons* in America.

While the earth shook and the mountains were being pushed up, lava flowed onto the surface. In some places volcanoes formed. Earthquakes and volcanoes are often signs of mountain building.

A few million years ago, giant sloths, small camels, saber-tooth tigers, and odd rhinoceroses made their homes in this area. The land was warm and wet.

As the Sierra Nevada rose, the climate changed. It got too cold for the animals. They died out. During this time, sequoias began growing on the mountains. While the sequoias grew, the mountains grew taller still.

The highest peak is now 14,495 feet high. On the gentle west slope grow thick green forests. Below the high, steep east side there is a desert.

One night in 1872, an earthquake shook the area. The mountains shifted, and walls of rock came tumbling down. It destroyed the little eastern town of Lone Pine on the desert floor beneath the mountains. Twenty-seven people were killed. When it was over, the mountains had grown by 13 feet. They may grow higher still.

WHAT SHAPES A MOUNTAIN?

Wind, rain, hot and cold temperatures, mountain streams, and glaciers change a mountain. Water seeps into cracks and freezes, causing rock to crumble. Each tiny fleck of rock is broken off and blown away, or carried down the mountain in streams, mud slides, or by avalanche.

Moss, *lichen,* and the roots of trees also help to crumble rock. Minute by minute, through millions of years, they change the mountain.

About two million years ago, *glaciers* formed. The earth was colder. The snow in the mountains did not melt in the summer. Year after year it piled up. It became so thick it changed into ice. Slowly this mass of ice started to move down the mountains.

FUN FACT The John Muir Trail, at the crest of the Sierra Nevada, covers 212 miles. It goes from Yosemite Park to Mount Whitney in Sequoia Park.

Wind, rain, hot and cold temperatures, water, and glaciers change the shape of a mountain.

As it moved, it was powerful enough to change things. Soft stone was ground into powder. Rock was picked up and huge piles were left in other places.

Glaciers scooped out river valleys, dug them deeper, and made them into wide, steep-walled canyons. They left many mountain peaks, some tall and jagged and others smooth and round. They filled in lakes and made new ones. Whole sides of mountains were cut away and their rivers now tumble over the edges as waterfalls.

Glaciers formed several different times. Each time they carved the mountains into new and different shapes. There are more than 70 peaks in Sequoia and Kings Canyon—all signs of the power of weather and glaciers.

CLIMBING MOUNT WHITNEY

Mount Whitney is the highest peak in Sequoia Park and the whole Sierra Nevada Range. It is a huge hunk of granite. Its peak and those next to it look

FUN FACT Three fishermen made the first climb of Mount Whitney in August 18, 1873. They were Albert Johnson, John Lucas, and Charles Begole.

like the pointy teeth of a giant. Still, people want to climb it! Although mountain climbers love to scale Mount Whitney's high, steep face, most people choose another way.

One way is to walk up. There is a safe, well-graded trail. People drive halfway up the mountain from Owens Valley on the east side. Then they hike up the rest of the 6,000 feet.

It is wise to wait a day and camp overnight until your body can adjust to the elevation. Mount Whitney is high, 14,495 feet high. The air is thin. There is less oxygen in it. Hikers should walk slowly, stop often, and enjoy the view. That is the only way to prevent altitude sickness. This happens when people try to climb too high, too fast. They get nausea and headaches, feel weak and lose their appetites. The only cure is rest. If that does not help, the person must be taken down to a lower elevation.

Every year, hundreds of people of all ages reach the *summit*. It takes three days to climb up and come back down. Along the way are places to

To prevent altitude sickness, hikers walk slowly and rest often.

The elephant head flower was named for its uniquely-shaped blooms.

camp. There are a few low streams to cross and the ground is rocky in some places.

WHAT IS IT LIKE ON TOP OF A MOUNTAIN?

All up and down the mountains the flowers bloom. In spring as the snow melts higher and higher up the mountains, flowers creep behind until they finally reach the top. Here tiny flowers hug the ground. They cling against the stark grey rock, dressed in gentle colors of pink, yellow, purple, and white. This is the *high Sierra,* the *arctic-alpine zone* of the mountains.

At the top of most mountains it is bone-chilling cold. But the high Sierra has pleasant weather in the summer. It is cool and a constant wind blows. Storms can come up quickly, so backpackers must be prepared. But storms rarely last more than an hour. Then the sun shines again.

There are hundreds of lakes. Tiny flowers sprinkle mountain *meadows.* There are yellow buttercups, mountain dandelions, pink fireweed, and pinkish-white pussy paws. The soil is thin. It is covered with rocks and boulders.

In wet meadows grows a flower called elephant head. It is a slender stem of pink and white blooms. Each little bloom looks like a tiny elephant head, with two big floppy ears and a tiny pink trunk. Up here there is another flower called steer's head. It looks like the bleached skull of a steer.

The top of Mount Whitney is like a cold, windy desert. It is too high for trees to grow. Animals like the yellow-bellied marmot (a groundhog), mountain sheep, and the rosy finch (a bird) live up here. Of course, wherever there are flowers, bumblebees and honeybees come to visit.

IN GIANT FOREST

Giant Forest is the heart of Sequoia National Park. Four of the five largest trees in the world grow here. Nowhere do sequoia trees grow as large as they do in this grove. Even the meadows are big, blooming all summer long with flowers. Around the meadows tower the trees. Giant Forest remains much

FUN FACT The first women to climb Mount Whitney were Mary Martin, Anna Mills, Hope Broughton, and Mrs. R. C. Redd on October 3, 1878.

as it was when John Muir named it more than 100 years ago. It has many thousands of sequoias.

Crescent Meadow is the largest meadow in Giant Forest. John Muir called it the "Gem of the Sierra" because of its beautiful flowers. Each week different kinds of flowers bloom. In June, Jeffrey shooting stars dot the meadow with lavender blooms. Later, a flower called Queen Anne's lace will cover the meadow with white. Bright yellow monkey flowers, red Indian paint brush, wild onions, and cow parsnips all bloom in their season.

Hale D. Tharp built his cabin in the fallen, burned-out log of a sequoia tree.

FUN FACT John Muir was a famous, Scottish-born naturalist who wrote much about the mountains. He started the Sierra Club, a club concerned with saving wilderness areas. He lived in Yosemite Park where his mountain cabin still stands.

Cutting a tunnel through a fallen sequoia was easier than trying to move it!

Creeks flow in the meadows and tiny trout idle in the streams. Easy walking trails circle around so visitors can admire the view. Many other trails lead out of this area for backpackers and mountain climbers. The High Sierra Trail starts here. It goes to Mount Whitney through 70 miles of deep canyons and rugged mountains.

In Giant Forest are two old cabins. One is Tharp's Log. In 1858, Hale D. Tharp, a rancher, was the first white man to enter Giant Forest. He came back each summer for 30 years. He brought his horses and cattle to graze in the meadows. He built a cabin in a fallen, burned-out log of a sequoia tree. The log was fitted with a door, window, stone fireplace, and furniture.

FUN FACT In Giant Forest are trees with all kinds of strange names. Room Tree is a tree that has been hollowed out by fire. It can hold 25 people or more!

The other cabin was built by another settler. When he found out Tharp already owned the land, he left his cabin and moved on.

There is a fallen tree on which people can drive their cars called Auto Log. There is a Tunnel Log, too. In 1937, a sequoia tree fell over the road and a tunnel was cut through it. That was easier than moving the tree! The tunnel is wide so cars can drive through. When the trees are standing, it is hard to understand how very tall they are. But these two downed trees help people feel their immense size.

Congress Trail is one of the most popular walking trails in Giant Forest. Here stand the House and Senate Groups. They are groups of trees that have been named in honor of our government. Some are named for our presidents, such as the Lincoln and the Washington tree. There is also a tree called the Chief Sequoyah.

Sequoyah belonged to the Cherokee tribe. He invented an alphabet for his people. He was known and respected throughout the world. After the trees were discovered, *botanists* argued for years over what to call them. Finally the name *Sequoia gigantea* was agreed upon. The name honors the man Sequoyah. It means giant sequoia trees.

MORO ROCK

Within Giant Forest is an immense granite mass called Moro Rock. It was formed 100 million years ago. Since then wind, rain, and freezing cold have weathered it smooth, much like a bald head. All that remains is a rounded dome of hard granite.

Moro Rock rises 4,000 feet above the Middle Fork of the Kaweah River. It is a good spot from which to view Giant Forest. On clear days, people who climb the 350 dizzying steps can see down to the San Joaquin Valley below. To the south is a deep canyon through which the Kaweah River winds. To the east tower the peaks of the Great Western Divide.

From Moro Rock, all the different life zones in the park can be seen. At the bottom are the foothills of the Sierra. Here the trees are sparse and the ground covered with brush. In the middle of the mountain are thick forests of fir, pine, and sequoia. At the very top of the mountains is the *alpine* zone. Trees thin out until they do not grow at all. Up there the wind is sharp and cold. The air is thin and the sunlight intense. Few plants grow. The summer

FUN FACT Just the first branch of the General Sherman is about 130 feet long. The trunk of that branch is seven feet thick. If it stood upright, it would be taller and larger than most of the trees people have in their yards.

350 steps lead to the top of Moro Rock—and to a spectacular view.

is too short.

Someone once said that these parks are like three worlds—a world of silent forest, a world of savage canyons, and a world of wind-swept granite peaks. From the top of Moro Rock you can see all three worlds.

CRYSTAL CAVE

Not all the wonders of Giant Forest are above the ground. About a half-mile down a very steep trail, past a waterfall, past nutmeg trees, is a cave. It has an iron gate shaped like a spider web. But there are very few spiders in Crystal Cave.

Long, flowing stone icicles, called *stalactites,* hang from the ceiling. Growing up from the cave floor are *stalagmites,* formed by water dripping on the same spot for thousands of years. There are curtains of stone and formations that look like bacon strips.

All were made in the same way. Water from rain and snow seeped down through the ground into the dry cave. Over thousands of years different shapes were formed. Some of the shapes resemble animals or people.

In one room is a huge block of marble that fell to the floor a long time ago. Now it looks like a gigantic cake over which someone has poured frosting.

A creek flows through the cool, damp cave. There are many rooms. In one room a guide will turn off the lights to show people how dark it really is.

Wildlife sometimes enters and leaves the cave. A bat flies in now and then. A bear may den up in cold weather in some of the outer openings of the cave. Even the bones of a deer have been found. Except for millipedes, a tiny dark spider species, and a few mice, very few animals care to live inside. Still it is a great place to explore.

HOW TO BE SAFE IN THE MOUNTAINS

In the tourist areas, the parks are very safe. But most of Kings Canyon and Sequoia Park is rugged mountain country. *Mountaineers* have made a

FUN FACT No matter how old the trees are, they contine to grow and add new wood to their trunks every year. In just the last 40 years, the General Sherman has added enough new wood to its trunk to build a house.

list of things that you should carry if you go hiking for a day or more in the backcountry. They are called the "ten essentials" because they can mean the difference between life and death.

1. Clothing. The sun is more harmful high on top of a mountain. Wear or bring long-sleeve shirts, slacks or jeans, a brimmed hat, a light jacket, a wool sweater, and extra clothing.
2. Food and *extra* food in case you are hurt or lost.
3. Sunglasses (lip salve and sunburn cream might be needed, too).
4. A Boy Scout-type knife.
5. Fire starters, such as a few candle stubs.
6. Matches in a waterproof container.
7. First-aid kit including moleskin for blisters.
8. Flashlight with an extra bulb and batteries.
9. Map.
10. Compass.

There are other things needed: a sleeping bag and ground cover, a backpack, a canteen (a quart size is a must for carrying water), good sturdy shoes and extra socks (damp socks lead to blisters). A whistle may come in handy. All backpackers must have a park permit to sleep overnight.

What are some dangers?

Backpackers face many dangers when hiking in the backcountry. With planning and proper equipment, many of these hazards can be avoided. The more common dangers facing backpackers are:

Running water—The most frequent cause of death in Sequoia and Kings Canyon is people falling into waterfalls or fast moving, cold mountain streams.

Hypothermia—This happens when the body loses too much heat. Older names for this condition were "exposure" and "freezing to death." If you get wet and there is a wind, hypothermia can happen even when the temperature isn't below freezing.

Falling off a cliff—If you fall, wait for rescuers.

Falling rocks—It is better for the victim to remain still and wait for help. Be calm. Others in the party should stay with the hurt person.

Getting lost—Sit down, don't panic, make camp, eat. Wait to be rescued. If you carry a whistle, use it now. (Before you even go hiking, make sure someone knows your plans in case you don't return on schedule.)

Bad weather—Strong winds, a sudden snowstorm, and rain can mean

FUN FACT   Kings Canyon is deeper than the Grand Canyon, but not as long.

Because of people like John Muir, the giant sequoias survived possible extinction.

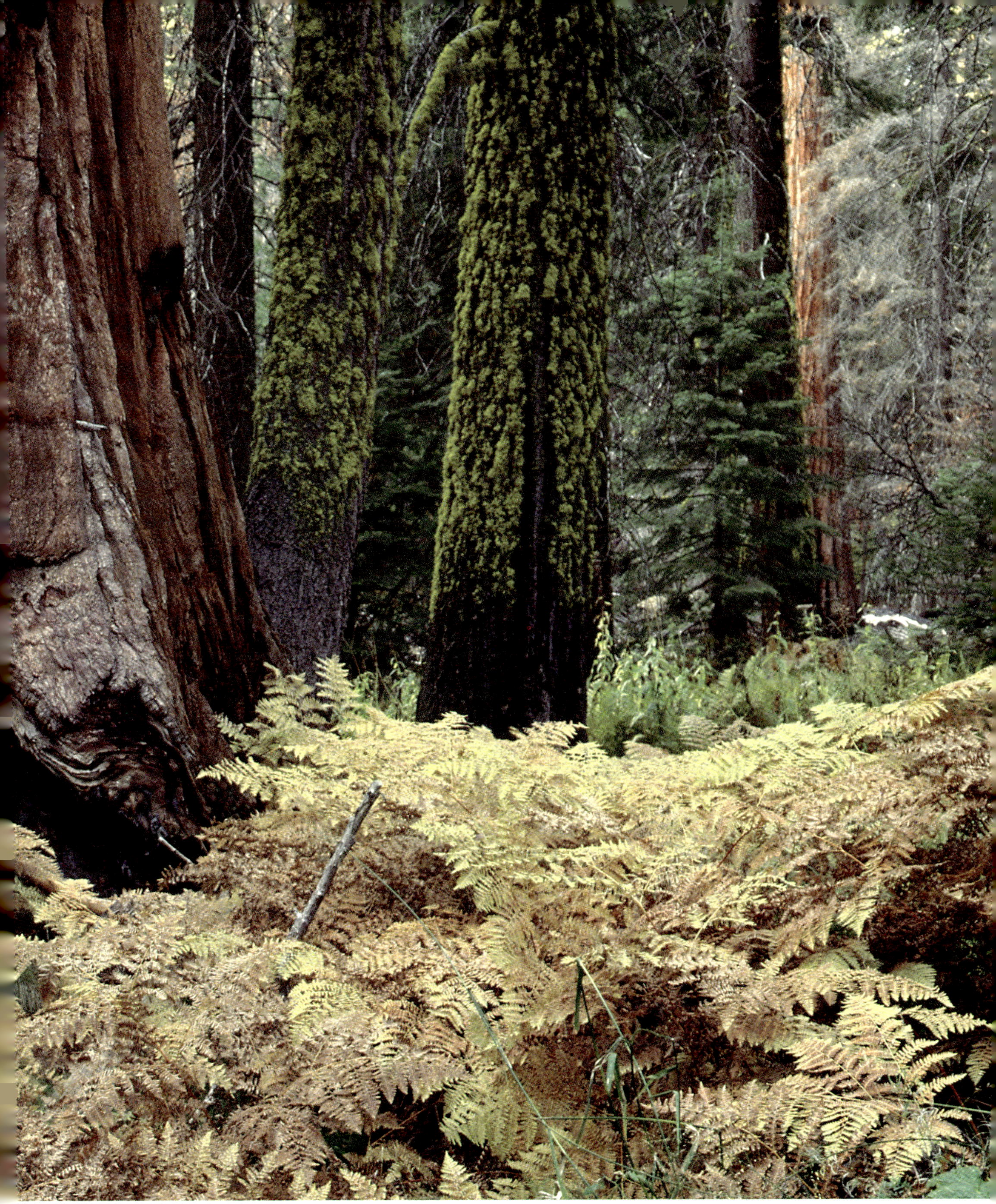

slippery trails, sudden darkness, hypothermia, and mud slides. Lightning is frequent in the mountains. Take cover.

Bears, snakes, and insects—Store all food in trees, never in your tent. This will keep bears away from your tent, and your food will be safe. Stay on the trails. Learn where snakes live. Carry insect repellent.

Thirst—Take a quart of water for each person, even on short walks. If you must use water from a stream, boil it for five minutes before you drink it.

THINGS TO DO

There are fun things to do and see at both Sequoia and Kings Canyon National Parks. Here are a few ideas:

Visit Giant Forest or Grant Grove. Walk beneath the giants. Ranger stations, campgrounds, stables, and food are close by.

Picnic near a wildflower meadow.

Take a guided tour with a ranger-naturalist to learn about the animals, wildflowers, and giant sequoias.

Climb Moro Rock.

Camp overnight. Be sure to have a permit.

See pictographs and mortar holes that were left behind at Potwisha and Hospital Rock.

Visit Crystal Cave.

Catch a golden trout in a mountain stream.

Cross-country ski, snowshoe, or sled in winter.

Rent a horse and trot away down a well-marked trail.

SAYING GOODBYE AND HELLO

Just outside of Kings Canyon National Park is a huge graveyard of giant sequoia stumps. It is all that remains of what used to be one of the largest sequoia groves. During the 1800s this forest was wiped out by lumber companies.

The quiet beauty of sequoias and the vastness of a wilderness area can be found in Sequoia and Kings Canyon National Parks.

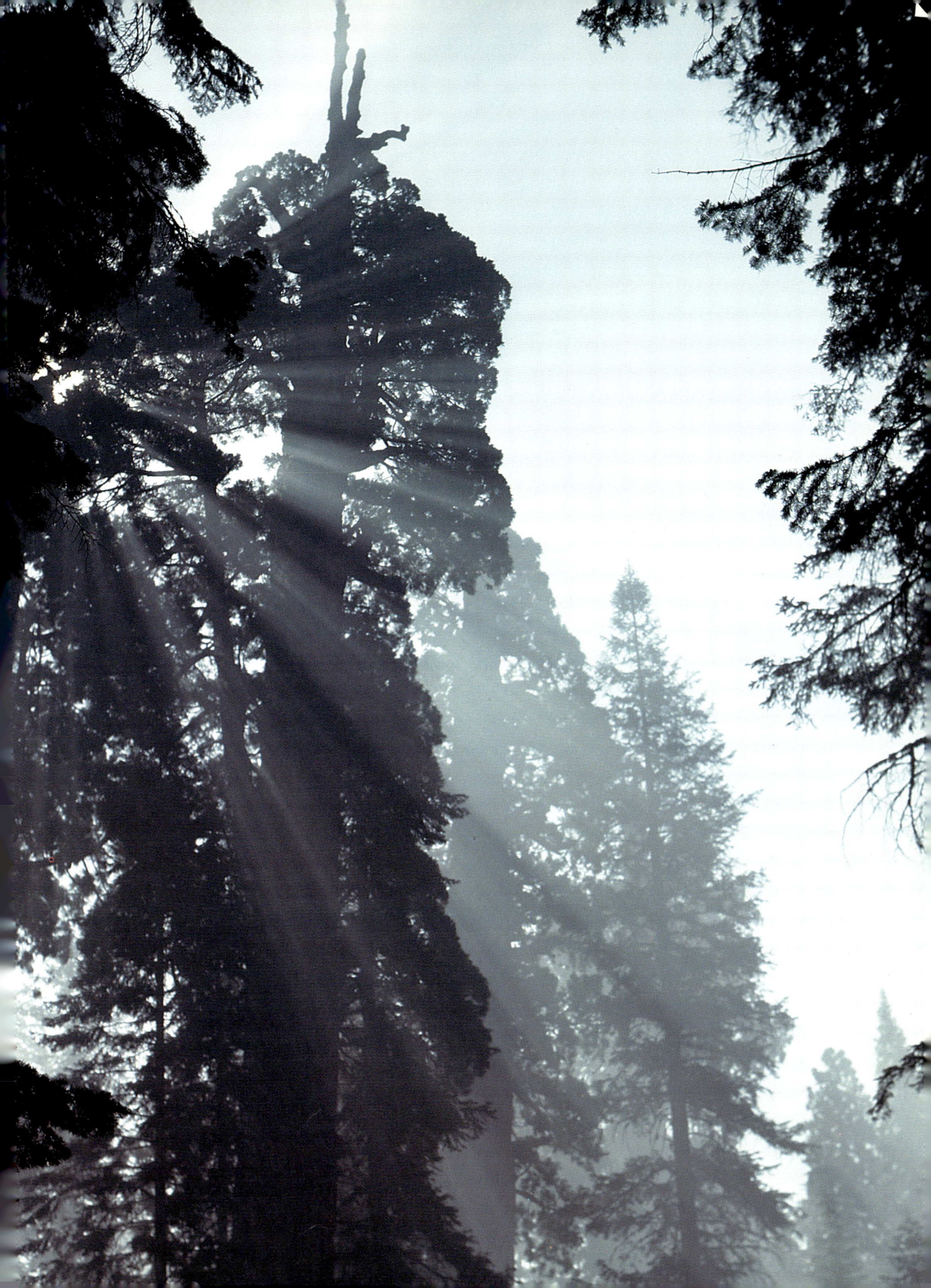

In this 2,600-acre grove only one tree was left standing. It was the largest tree in the the grove, 35-feet thick at the base. Maybe it was just too thick to cut. It stands out starkly against the sky, one lone tree overlooking the Canyon of the Kings River.

This living monument reminds people of the destruction that was done. Its name is the Boole Tree. Some people are surprised by its name, since Frank A. Boole was the man in charge of cutting down all the trees.

Today, rising within the waste of this forest are thousands of young saplings. They show the spirit of a species that was here long before this country began. They show the spirit of people who care about mountains, waterfalls, deep canyons, wildflowers, mountain sheep, and giant trees.

FOR MORE PARK INFORMATION

For more information about Sequoia and Kings Canyon, write to:

Sequoia and Kings Canyon National Parks
Three Rivers, CA 93271

FUN FACT The Boole tree is 35 feet thick. Would your house or apartment fit in such a tree?

PARK MAP

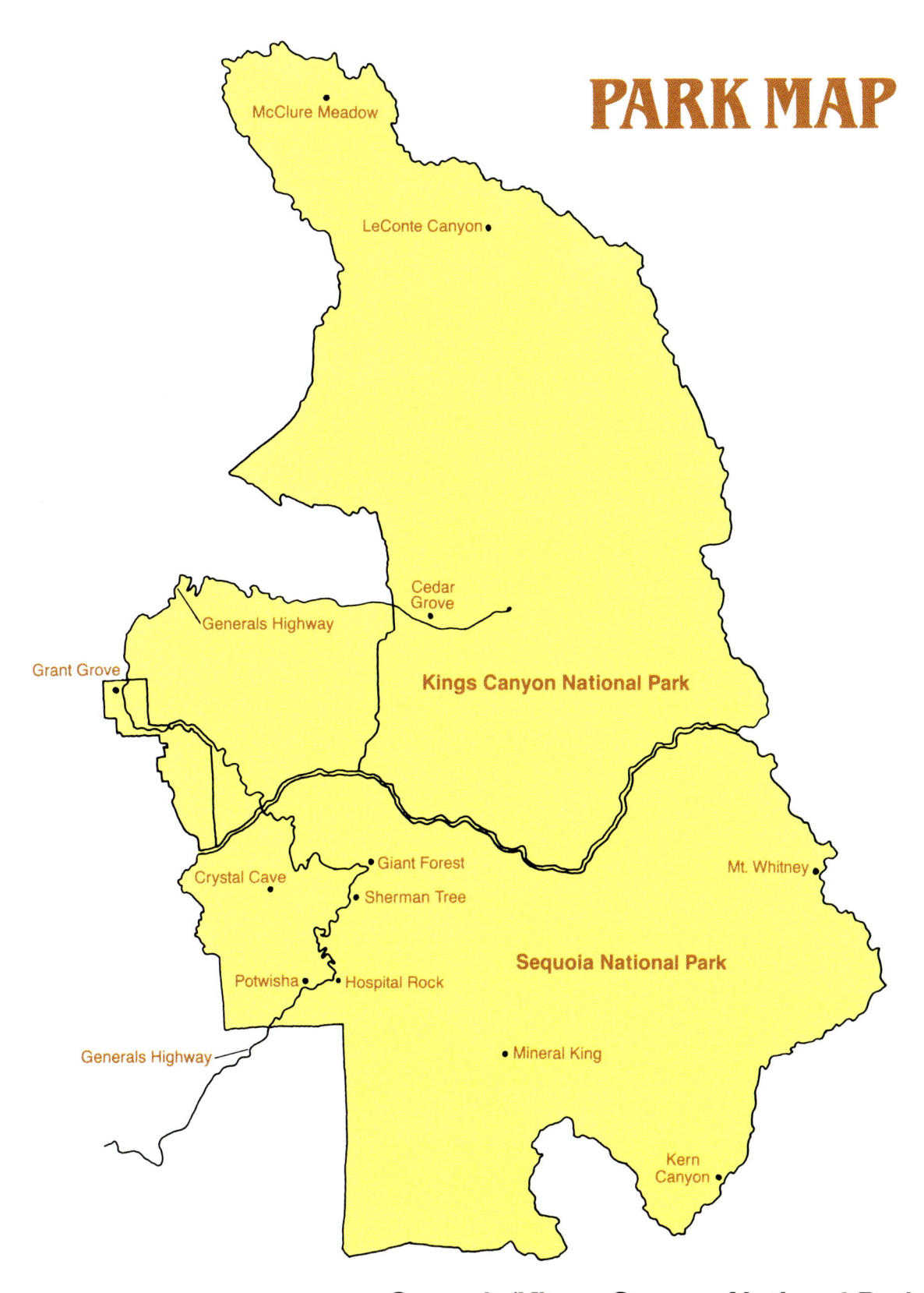

Sequoia/Kings Canyon National Parks

GLOSSARY/INDEX

ALPINE *36*—Referring to high mountains.

ARCTIC-ALPINE ZONE *33*—The highest part of a mountain, where trees can no longer grow.

BATHOLITH *26*—A large mass of hardened volcanic rock under the earth's crust that is more than 40 miles long and has no known floor.

BOTANIST *36*—A person who studies plants.

CANYON *6, 29, 30, 38, 44*—A narrow valley with steep cliff walls formed by running water; U-shaped valleys are cut out by glaciers.

CONTROLLED BURNINGS *10*—The park's program to use fire to promote the growth of certain plants; it keeps the forest healthy and brings back wildlife to the area.

ERODE *16*—To wear away.

FORMATIONS *38*—Rock shapes formed when water drips inside a cave, and leaves behind deposits of calcium carbonate.

FOSSIL *16*—A print of ancient life that has been embedded in rock.

GLACIER *16, 29, 30*—A huge body of ice moving slowly down a mountain slope or valley.

GRANITE *26, 29, 30, 36, 38*—A rock formed by magma that cools and hardens within the earth.

HABITAT *26*—An area where a plant or animal normally lives.

HAMMERSTONE *19*—A heavy stone used as a hammer.

HIGH SIERRA *33*—The high mountain terrain of the Sierra Nevada mountain range.

LICHEN *29*—Crust-like, scaly, or branching growth on rocks or tree trunks.

MAGMA *26*—Molten rock deep in the earth.

MEADOW *8, 10, 22, 33, 34, 35, 42*—An area of grassland in its natural state.

MORTAR *19, 42*—A hole in a rock into which food was placed to be crushed or ground with the aid of a pestle.

MOUNTAINEERS *38*—One who climbs mountains for sport; a native or inhabitant of a mountain.

OBSIDIAN *20*—A volcanic glass, usually black, that can be chipped into arrowheads.

OUZEL *24, 25, 26* — A grey water bird.

PETRIFIED FOREST *16* — A forest where wood (and other organic matter) has turned into stone.

PICTOGRAPH *19, 42* — Pictures painted on rocks by prehistoric people.

PREHISTORIC *16, 19* — The time before the history of a people was written.

SAPLING *11, 44* — A young tree.

SEEDLING *10, 15* — A young plant or tree that is grown from a seed.

SEQUOIA GIGANTEA *36* — The scientific name for sequoia trees, it means "giant sequoia".

STALACTITE *38* — An icicle-shaped rock hanging from the roof of a cave caused by dripping mineral-rich water.

STALAGMITE *38* — An icicle-shaped rock growing upward from the floor of a cave caused by the dripping of mineral-rich water.

SUMMIT *31* — The highest point or peak of a mountain.

TAP ROOT *15* — A primary root that grows straight down and gives off smaller roots.

UPTHRUST *29* — A great pressure that pushes mountains upward.

VALLEY *29, 30* — A long, narrow lowland between mountains carved by the erosion of a river.